My Love Letters Don't Sound The Same Anymore

a poetry memoir

cassandra grace

For the boy who broke my heart.

Because, the truth is,

I couldn't have done this without you.

But also,

for Rachel and Sarah,

who let me talk about my heartbreak

as much as I needed to.

And for Natalie,

who lovingly encouraged me to

"find a hobby that doesn't include men."

Contents

A Note from the Author   VIII

1. Preface: Selfish   1

2. Irony   2

3. Distancing   3

4. Vulnerability   4

5. Perspective   5

6. Restraint   6

7. Soul Mates   7

8. Object Permanence   8

9. Sunshine   9

10. Stay   10

11. Proposal   11

12. Lovely   12

13. Home   13

14. Confidence   14

15. Doubts   16

16. Blindsided   17

17. Questions   18

18. Fiancé   20

19. Symphonies   21

20. Gifts Ungiven   22

21. Anticipation   23

22. Relativity   24

23. Doors   25

24. Fear of Rejection   26

25. Incompatibility   28

26. Choices   29

27. Memory   30

28. Goodbyes   31

29. Home (Reprise)   32

30. Hollow   33

31. Fading   34

32. Confession   35

33. Heartache   36

34. Careful   37

35. Timeless   38

36. Farewell   39

37. Epilogue   40

Acknowledgements   42

About the Author   44

A Note from the Author

It's a strange thing to revisit a story that I not only wrote, but lived, years ago. With the passage of time and a lot of intentional healing, the events in this book seem strangely distant, more like a dream than a lived memory.

That being said, I know that sharing my experience with love and heartbreak has been encouraging and hopeful for many who read the first edition. It is my hope that that this second edition will serve you just as well.

And so, I ask again, dear reader, that you keep in mind this is only my side of the story. As a Christian, I had difficulty finding content about breakups that I could relate to. Though I'd been hurt, I did not hate; I wanted to heal, not just move on. Most secular media does not portray this kind of a response to a broken heart. And as much as Christians love to discuss "dating with purpose" and getting married, there is a strange silence when it comes to breakups.

This little book is an alternative response to breakups. I believe there are a large number of relationships that end simply because things didn't work out. And if that's your breakup story, you don't have to villainize your ex so you can feel better about what you lost. You don't have to justify your sadness. Let the situation be nothing more than what it is—and nothing less. Whether your heartbreak is a result of a messy or mundane breakup, allow yourself to grieve what you've lost. And allow that to take time. Grief is not a "cry once and move on" item to cross off a list. It's a process. Let yourself process it. I strongly recommend doing so alongside the caring love of Jesus. He knows better than anyone else how to help you through this time.

That being said, this author's note is the closest this book will come to giving you advice on dealing with your breakup. It is not my aim in this story to give you a solution to your pain and solve your problems. But, it is my hope that this story will give you permission to honestly grieve what you've lost. And in doing so, come to find healing.

Preface: Selfish

I think this will end up being
more for my benefit.
Helping me process
and understand what's going on, since,
apparently,
I can't understand emotions
unless they're translated into
written words
first.

So,
that being said,
this is probably not a collection
of love letters and soft words.
It's probably, more so,
a jumble
of insecurities and doubts,
hopes and dreams,
And really,
just a mess.
But that's me.
And that's life.

Irony

The first words of my
first love letter
sound ironic now:

"Writing this
is a bit dangerous
because I am so honest
on paper.
But there's so much I want to tell you
and I'm not good at goodbyes."

In fact, all my letters to you
now seem riddled with foreshadowing
and double meaning.
As though
even when I was happy and in love, I was
already grieving you.

Distancing

I don't think I'm very good
at long distance.
It hurts so badly when
I miss you
that my brain represses it completely.
I know
I miss you,
But I don't feel
that I do.

It's your photos
and your sweatshirt that remind me
you are real.
Because sometimes
when I try to remember you,
I can't remember what it feels like
to hold your hand,
or to be held by you,
or to kiss you.
And in those moments,
it's harder than it should be
to remember that
you actually exist.
You aren't just a dream.
And I try not to be frustrated with myself,
because I know my brain is only trying
to protect me
from the pain of missing you.

Vulnerability

I love you.
I want to trust you.
I do trust you.

Don't let me be wrong
in deciding to trust you,
in deciding to love you.

Perspective

I wish you could see yourself
the way I do.
You're such a wonderful person.

And don't worry,
I know you're not perfect.
I'm not closing my eyes
so you can look like the person
I want you to be.
I see you
as you are.
And to say you're incredible
is an understatement.

Let me believe in you
until you are able
to see it
for yourself.

Restraint

In my heart,
I'm so certain
that I see my future with you.
Yet, I can't help but try to sound
reasonable,
because there's just enough
uncertainty
that I feel like
I need to cushion my enthusiasm,
just in case
this does crumble.

Soul Mates

I don't believe
there is such a thing as
"The One."
I know that soul mates don't
really exist.
But that makes this
all the more lovely to me.
That you love me
not because fate declared you would,
or the stars aligned
and said it would be so.
But you love me
just because
you choose to.

There is no one else for me but you.
Not because another
doesn't exist,
but because I have decided
that you are enough.
You are all I need.
You are everything I want.

Object Permanence

I have a tendency to forget
about people
If I'm not with them
all the time.
But it's impossible to forget
about you.

Sunshine

The nice weather lately
makes me think of you.
I think the optimism and liveliness that
spring and summer bring
are similar to the way I feel
when I'm with you.
And because the weather
makes me happy,
I just want to sit outside with you,
so you can feel
the happy weather too.
I just want to share everything good
I find
and have
with you.

Stay

I've tried to think about it.
To entertain the idea
of letting you go.
I prayed for God
to reveal it to me, if
that's what I need to do,
and to give me the strength
to leave you.

But I won't.
I don't need to.
The only reason you have
is that you think I deserve
better.
That's not reason enough.
Not when I know
I will continue to choose you.
Not when I see
how much you love me,
even as you tell me to
leave you.

Please
don't push me away.
Not when
we both want to stay.
Not when
there is no justifiable reason
to let go.

Proposal

I know
it's too soon.
I know
that I don't know
anything about love yet.
But I really could marry you.
I know about commitment
and sticking to my word,
and I'm willing to see whatever may come
with you.
As naïve as that may be,
as stupid as it may seem,
if you asked me,
I would say yes.

Lovely

I love you dearly.
And, my dear,
you are lovely.
When I look at you,
I remember
there is good in the world,
right in front of me.

Home

I'm not letting you go.
I love you.
So much.
And hopefully someday
relatively soon,
you won't have to leave
to go home anymore.
Because home
will be with me.

Confidence

When I think about my future,
there are no hopes or wishes
that you'll be a part of it.
Your presence in my life
is a given.
There is assurance in it.
I see you there
with comfortable certainty.
The way I'm certain
the grass is green
and the sky is blue.
It's a constant,
a fact I don't have to remind myself
is true.

But unlike the grass
and the sky,
I am humbled
and grateful
for the confidence I have in you.
Chlorophyll
doesn't have the option
to change its mind and reflect
a different color.
But any day,
for any reason,
you could decide
I'm not someone you want in your life
anymore.

I'm reminded with each stroke of my pen
that makes my thoughts public and undeniable,
that there will always be the chance
you won't reciprocate.
I am reminded that
my comfortable certainty
is not a guarantee
you have the same confidence
in me.

Doubts

For the first time, just now,
I start to wonder
if we'll actually make it.
I've always known losing you was
possible,
but I never thought it
plausible.
And there's nothing that's happened
to make me think
we will
or
we should
break up now.
But I also know
how quickly relationships can change.

Hold on to me.
Don't let me lose you.
I...
I should call you.

Blindsided

Was it ironic
that you broke up with me
the weekend I thought
you were going to propose?

Or was I
just that stupid?

Questions

Before we even dated, you asked me
to marry you.
Before we even kissed,
you asked again
if I would marry you.
When we got serious about the possibility
of marriage, you stopped asking.
Because you bought a ring,
and the next time you asked
would be the real thing.

A month later, you told me
to pick a day next year.
You hadn't officially asked yet.
But it felt like
an unofficial engagement.

You had been planning to do it the next week,
but decided people would say,
"It's too soon."
I had to remind myself that
despite how close we were,
I wasn't engaged until I was engaged.

So a month after that,
I drove eight hours to see you.
Every day,
you took me to a beautiful place.

You never asked though,
and I figured you were just trying to
keep me on my toes.

I drove eight hours back
to a home far away from you,
only to drive
eight hours back to you
two days later.

I knew something was wrong.
I thought it was just in your head.
But it didn't go away,
so I asked you
to talk to me.
You asked
if I thought we were too different.

Three days later,
you broke up with me.
So, I drove eight hours back
to a home far away from you,
knowing I might never see
those roads
or you
again.

Fiancé

It's funny,
because I had just told my mom
I was tired of telling people:
"I'm going to Ohio
to visit my boyfriend."

This is not what I meant.
But I guess wishes
are tricky like that.

Symphonies

If there's one thing I'll never forget, it's
the way you sang to me.
Like maybe life could be
a bit more magical if we just
opened our eyes
and tuned our ears to the
symphony playing all around us.
Maybe I, too, can learn
to sing along, even if
you are no longer here
to teach me how.

Gifts Ungiven

He bought me a ring,
so I wrote him a song.
It was going to be
a beautiful exchange.
But I never got to wear it,
and he never got to hear it.
Instead,
I took off the bracelet with his initial,
and he listened to me cry.

Anticipation

I was sad,
but honestly,
also a little relieved
that you'd gone.
I think waiting for the goodbye,
anticipating you leaving,
was almost as draining
as the actual goodbye.
I trust that means
it was the right thing for you
to go.

Relativity

You were worried we wouldn't have anything
to keep us together
once the honeymoon phase was over.
And that "spark" for you
had already died.
I guess you assumed
it was only a matter of time
that mine would too.
But after all that time, I
only loved you more.
I only found you more beautiful and lovely
with the passage of time.

So what happened in the time between,
that what only grew for me
only faded for you,
when it had seemed like we had experienced
the same thing
at the same time?

Doors

I don't crack open doors
I have no desire to walk through.
I knew what I was getting into with you.
I chose it.
Knowingly.
Purposefully.
Falling in love with you
wasn't an accident.
I chose you.
And you chose me too,
for a time.

But I guess you got tired of my company,
so you walked me back to the door,
asked me to step outside--
just for a moment.
I don't crack open doors
I have no desire to walk through.
But you opened this one for me,
so what choice did I have?
I turned back, hoping,
at least,
for a doorway conversation,
but with tears in your eyes,
you closed it on me.

Fear of Rejection

You would cry
when I kissed you.
Because, you said,
no one had ever loved you the way I did.
And it baffled you
how I could love you so much
when I'd never been in love before.
Even so, you were terrified
I'd leave you;
told me to leave,
because you didn't deserve me.

Of course, I didn't walk away.
I loved you,
tried to hold on to you.
All I wanted
was for you to be grateful.
To find relief that
for once
someone wouldn't abandon you.

I chose you
over and over again.
And you said
no one had ever loved you like that.

But even so,
you stopped choosing me.

And because I love you,
the only thing I could do was
let you go.
But I hope you remember that
I never gave up
on you.

Incompatibility

I try to remind myself
that this is for the better.
That I need someone whose values
are just a little more aligned
with mine.
That I need a man who
loves God, not just
acknowledges Him.
But that can change,
and then you'd be perfect.

But I can't build a life on
possibilities.
I had tried to tell you
that your future begins
now.
The person you want to be
then
is the person you have to start to be
today.

Because if I can only judge who you will be
based on who you are, then
you aren't right
for me.

Choices

I spent so much time
loving you,
choosing you,
so grateful that you let me be
a part of your life
that I have to remind myself
not loving you
is also a choice.
Yet somehow,
despite everything,
that one is so much harder to do.

Memory

I'm forgetting again.
What it feels like to be in your presence.
How comfortable it actually is
to have you around.
I forget so quickly
and so easily.
But what I do remember—
when I'm able to—
is so vivid
it almost hurts more
than the forgetting.

Goodbyes

I don't think we said anything.
We never really do.
Neither of us are great at goodbyes.
But I remember
you complimented my sweatshirt,
because it was yours.
I remember
I couldn't say much
of anything,
because if I did,
I'd just have asked you to stay.

As you turned to walk
back to your car,
I could only stand there
and watch
until you were far enough away
that I wouldn't try to close the distance.
Because if I'd moved my feet,
it wouldn't have been to go back inside,
but instead
to run to you
and hold you close
and beg you to stay
one more night.

Home (Reprise)

My heart physically hurts.
I desired
nothing more
than that you would be
the person I came home to,
or who came home to me,
for the rest of my life.

Hollow

It feels a bit
empty
without you.
The way a house is empty
when you've been home alone for a while.
It's still familiar.
Still comfortable.
But it's quiet and still,
missing
a bit of life.

I miss you already.

Fading

To say I'm forgetting you
isn't quite right.
Goodness knows I think of you
quite often.
But I'm forgetting
what it's like to be with you.
Almost like all of our time together
was a dream,
and it didn't actually happen
to me.

Confession

I can't help but feel
a little guilty about moving on.
I can't help but taste
the bitter-sweetness
of letting you go.
Of realizing you are now
a stranger
I once knew.

I can't help feeling like
I need to ask your forgiveness,
as though in some way
I've given up on you.
But I know that all you'll feel
upon my confession
is relief
that I'm no longer holding on to
what could have been
with you.

I still wish nothing but the best for you,
but I see now,
I'm no longer part of that.

Heartache

It hasn't gotten better.
Missing you.
Usually it's unbearable,
but only for a moment,
and then I go numb to it.
My brain blocks it out.

But lately,
it keeps hurting more
and I feel it more often.
I feel it all the time.
I lie in bed and sob without tears
because I miss you
so much.

I feel I'm at war with myself.
Part of me aches
and wants nothing more than
to be near you.
Another part of me
is trying to block that out.
Ignore it.

I just don't know
how to properly process emotions,
So they get all tangled up in my head.
Maybe I'm getting too in my head
about everything.
I just need to see you,
to know it's all going to be okay.

Careful

I know
if I'm not careful
I'll lie awake for hours
thinking about
what could have been
instead of what could be.

And I'll forget
that I'm happy now,
in spite of everything.
And I'll forget
how happy I will be
with someone else.

Timeless

I meant every word I've said to you.
I've never lied to you.
I trust you.
I love you.
And if there was only
one person
who could be guaranteed to be there
for the rest of my life,
I would choose you.
Without a doubt.
In a heartbeat.
With all your bad days.
With all your flaws.
I'd still choose you
every time.

Farewell

I hope the days pass easily
until I see you again.
You are always in my thoughts.
I love you,
dearly.

Epilogue

Although I am leaving you and moving on,
please know, it's not because
I think less of you
or no longer love you,
or am abandoning you.

Our chapter is simply
over.
The ink for our pages has run out.
Dried up.

I will cherish the words
that were written there,
but it's just a story now.

Acknowledgements

When I first released *My Love Letters Don't Sound the Same Anymore,* I had little idea what I was doing, and for some reason, attempted to do it nearly all on my own.

But with this second edition, I find there are many more people I owe my thanks to.

Thank you to my mom, who edited the first edition, as well as the second. Who sat with me in my heartbreak and reminded me it wasn't the end. And who has encouraged me with every story I've written.

Thank you to Maggie for creating such a beautiful cover for this second edition.

Thank you to my re-launch team: Staci, Julie, Linda, Con, Erica, and Sarah. Thank you for believing in me and this book.

Thank you to the indie authors before me who have given me insight into the indie publishing process, namely, Erin Phillips, and Alissa J. Zavalianos.

And above all, thank you to Jesus, who provides love like no other. To my Heavenly Father, who has set all things perfectly into place. And to the Holy Spirit, who has equipped me to tell this story in its time and given me many more stories to tell yet.

About the Author

Cassandra Grace knew she wanted to be an author when she was in second grade. Although her career path has taken a few detours since then, she's pleased to have returned to her love of storytelling. Whether it be poetry, songs, fantasy, biblical retellings, or nonfiction, if it's a story worth telling, she'll find the right genre to tell it.

Cassandra lives in the American Midwest because, honestly, nothing beats a farm view and a casserole (except, perhaps, a good book).

You can find more about Cassandra Grace and her upcoming projects at www.cassandraspocket.net